CW00685741

A Marvelous Life

IS WHERE
YOU ARE HEADED

Written by Joey Lynn Butler

Designed by Dayna Elefant

A special thank you to cover photographer, Bahman Farzad.
Your unparalleled eye and talent has left a beautiful legacy for us all.

Dedicated to all who have encouraged
me to fly...let's soar!

These words could not have been put to paper without my precious daughter, Sophie. I never knew I could love like this, until the day you and Boden were born. Now take this book and "GO GET 'EM!" You are destined for greatness.

To my Mom and biggest cheerleader, Sharon. And to my Dad, Jeff. Thank you for seeing the light in me and treating me as if that's all you see.

To Marci, "Young" Dave and my favorite teacher, Matt. You make the world a better place by being in it. I love you three.

To Dayna, the designer of this book. Your passion, energy and light is simply magnetic!

UNDERSTANDING CHANGE...

A move, a new job, a change in an educational institute...you will run into many changes in your lifetime. Change can be both exciting and also stressful because with change we go from the familiar to the unfamiliar, which requires an adjustment. Please do not jump to the conclusion that any discomfort is evidence that you made the wrong choice. Allow for beautiful, new levels of responding to and experiencing your new environment. And allow for patience.

PLOT TWIST…

Sometimes life calls for a plot twist or change in direction. Give yourself permission to let go and GROW. It is very empowering to say, "This is no longer serving me." You are always allowed to start over…ALWAYS!

HUSTLE beats TALENT when talent no longer hustles.

If you get tired, learn to rest, not give up!

There are so many things you have that require no talent, but that can get you farther: PASSION, being COACHABLE, being PREPARED, ATTITUDE!!

Create your own personal vision statement in life that honors your values, strengths, and dreams...where you want to be and where you are headed.

A wonderful example of a personal vision is from

Richard Branson, founder of the Virgin Group:

"To have fun in my journey through life and learn from my mistakes."

To write your personal vision statement,

take out a piece of paper and:

1. Write down your values.

2. Describe your ideal self.

3. Identify what motivates you.

This will help guide you and help you

to make life decisions along the way!

Don't ever let fear win.

Participating in life makes you an absolute winner no matter what the outcome is. Never trust your fears...they don't know how strong you really are.

Being CALM is a SUPERPOWER!

Work your inner peace like a full-time job! Achieving serenity will change your life. To begin, realize you are not in control of others. Some places to find peace are in a morning routine, nature, connecting with God, meditation, journaling, or being creative.

Part of taking care of yourself is taking care of YOU mentally, physically, spiritually, and emotionally. Always strive for this beautiful balance.

Mama said there would be days like this...

(The Shirelles)

When times are tough, remember this is only temporary;

this too shall pass.

And remember this lovely quote by Hellen Keller:

"Although the world is full of suffering, it is also full of the OVERCOMING of it."

Expectations...

Expecting too much from others can lead to disappointment and resentment. Don't allow your happiness to depend on other people...remember, your happiness is an inside job.

Have high expectations for one person in particular—YOURSELF.

Stay away from high-risk individuals.

This is not meant to scare you, but stay away from people who are not trustworthy, who don't seem safe, who have values that are not in line with yours—in all of your relationships.

Remember: The best predictor of future behavior is past behavior. This means if you see something in someone that feels off, or witness a behavior that is not in line with your values, please pay attention and listen to your inner voice. Always listen to this inner voice. It is there to protect you.

To apologize is to be brave;
this takes courage—

It can be frightening not to
defend ourselves.

Learn the art of a good apology...

We all find ourselves having to apologize at one time or another.

A good apology consists of:

1. Acknowledging the person you are apologizing to.

2. Admitting that what you did caused hurt.

3. Apologizing.

4. Committing to change your behavior and keep your word!!!

Always buy Girl Scout cookies!

You have sold them before. You know how hard it is to sell them, and we need to support those TRAILBLAZERS! By selling cookies and participating, these young girls are developing a sense of self, practicing leadership skills, and learning how to thrive.

We want to support them; they are part of our future.

Dream, Dream Big, and Dream Often!

When you allow yourself to dream big, you discover your passions and what your purpose is here.

Big dreams are the reasons why your life or even the world changes for the better. They are the reason why there have been so many great achievements, inventions, and movements in this world. Big dreams give you the opportunity to truly reach your full potential and leave your mark in whatever area you choose.

Be a light in this world! There are so many ways to shine your light; it doesn't have to be huge...

Start by:

Giving a stranger a smile.

Calling your grandparents or parents just to say thank you.

Being a mentor...investing in someone who needs and wants your help.

Going to the grocery store for an elderly person.

Planting a garden with a child.

RELATIONSHIPS...
There is beauty in every relationship.

Some stay forever and some come to an end. The beauty is that there is a lesson in them all...some bring us healing, some teach us the importance of boundaries, some teach us how to love others and ourselves, and some teach us about forgiveness.

Never regret a past relationship and the gift you have received.

Never forget
how important
communication is.

Communicate even
when it's uncomfortable.
The worst distance
between two people is
a misunderstanding.

Upon waking, remember Gratitude.

Wake up every day and list five things you are grateful for. Melody Beattie said it best: "Gratitude can turn a meal into a feast, a house into a home and a stranger into a friend."

Remember to take care of YOURSELF.

It's not your job to be everything to everyone, and do everything for everyone.

When you get in the habit of putting everyone first, you teach them that you always come second.

"NO." is a
complete sentence.
Plain and simple.

You can be a good person with a kind and compassionate heart and still say NO.

Move on.

Don't waste time feeling sorry for yourself. And know when you move on, you aren't starting from scratch; you are starting from experience.

Don't let others control the course of your life.

Always place value on yourself, your goals, and your desires—and not so much on the expectations of what others want.

When you move
through life,
set intentions.

Call out what you desire. Through intention, we see more clearly, create more with passion, and actually manifest our desires. It is an amazing thing: One day you wake up and realize you are there—you have arrived!

It is more
than OK
to ask
for help!

We were not meant to do this life alone. If you are ever struggling, are sad, need a listening ear....please ask for help. You may think that asking for help makes you weak or means that there is something wrong with you. That couldn't be farther from the truth. Having the ability to ask for help is a sign of STRENGTH! And a sign of a healthy coping strategy. Whether it is a counselor, a trusted advisor, or someone you KNOW has your back, please always reach out. You will be sooo glad you did!

You are far too INCREDIBLE to be the only thing standing in your way!

Those pesky thoughts...There are a few things that we can control in life. Our thoughts are one of those things WE CAN CONTROL! Remember: You are what you think. Talk to yourself like you would to someone you love: a child, friend, or partner. This one thing can literally change your life.

When you are out at night or faced with a situation where you have a decision to make, go into the bathroom and ask yourself,

"When I wake up in the morning, which choice would make me the most proud of myself?"

And do that!

Adversity will surprise you when it shows up.

It will be someone you thought was a friend, or an area where you've traditionally excelled. Don't run. Turn and walk toward it—right toward it, even if it's inside you. Because if you don't, the same adversity will just keep finding you.

Taking care of
your body is
more important
now than ever...

In an article about living without regrets, Karl Pillemer stated, "Many people will say to themselves, 'I enjoy smoking' or 'I don't like to exercise' or 'I just like to eat—who cares if I die a little sooner?' The problem is in this day and age you're not going to die sooner; you're going to be stuck with 10 or 20 years of chronic disease as modern medicine keeps you alive."

Do your best to be sure the body you are in is the one that allows you to enjoy being alive.

Learn to fail
gracefully…

We all blow it at times. Even with our best effort we don't always get the A or make the team. We sometimes blow it with the wrong choice in a partner or the wrong decision.

When you realize things could have gone differently, get up, dust yourself off, cry a bit, feel those feelings and then get going. It is all just a learning experience.

If you are the smartest, most creative and highly evolved person in the room, you are in the wrong room!!!! Always surround yourself with people you can grow from, learn from and collaborate with.

Tomorrow is another good day. And Tomorrow's hope is that we have learned something from yesterday.

FOR A FRESH START, and to make the most of a new day:

1. Change up your routine. Say yes to a new experience.

   (For example, try a new yoga class.)

2. Put your phone down. Truly see the world around you.

   Take 15 minutes to people watch.

3. Become a tourist in your own city.

4. Make a new friend. Each person we invite to sit at our

   table of life brings his or her own unique perspective. While

   it might seem scary, put yourself out there and invite

   someone new into your world.